Rookie
Read-About® Holidays

Purim

D1521343

By Carmen Bredeson

Consultant
Don L. Curry
Reading and Content Consultant

Children's Press®
A Division of Scholastic Inc.
New York   Toronto   London   Auckland   Sydney
Mexico City   New Delhi   Hong Kong
Danbury, Connecticut

Designer: Herman Adler Design
Photo Researcher: Caroline Anderson
The photo on the cover shows different items used to celebrate Purim.

Library of Congress Cataloging-in-Publication Data

Bredeson, Carmen.
  Purim / by Carmen Bredeson.– 1st American ed.
      p. cm. – (Rookie read-about holidays)
Includes index.
Summary: An introduction to the Jewish holiday of Purim, which
commemorates Queen Esther of Persia and how she saved the Jews.
  ISBN 0-516-25880-X (lib. bdg.)   0-516-27928-9 (pbk.)
 1. Purim–Juvenile literature. [1. Purim. 2. Holidays.] I. Title. II.
Series.
  BM695.P8B72 2003
  296.4'36–dc21

                        2003004514

CHILDREN'S PRESS, and ROOKIE READ-ABOUT®,
and associated logos are trademarks and or registered trademarks
of Scholastic Library Publishing. SCHOLASTIC and associated logos
are trademarks and or registered trademarks of Scholastic Inc.

6 7 8 9 10 R 12 11   62

Do you celebrate
(SEL-uh-brate) Purim?

This holiday celebrates Esther. She was a Jewish woman who lived in Persia long ago.

Some people dress up as Esther on Purim.

פורים שמח

6

The king of Persia thought Esther was very beautiful. He made her his queen.

His name was King Achashverosh (ah-HASH-vay-ROSH). It is fun to dress like this king on Purim.

Queen Esther had an uncle named Mordechai (MORE-duh-kye). He was a very wise man.

He helped Queen Esther a lot. Once, he helped save the king's life.

Some people dress up as Mordechai on Purim.

9

10

Haman was one of the
king's men. He wore
a hat with three points.

Haman hated the Jewish people and wanted to kill them. Esther heard about Haman's plans.

She asked the king to help. Esther, Mordechai, and the king saved the Jewish people from Haman.

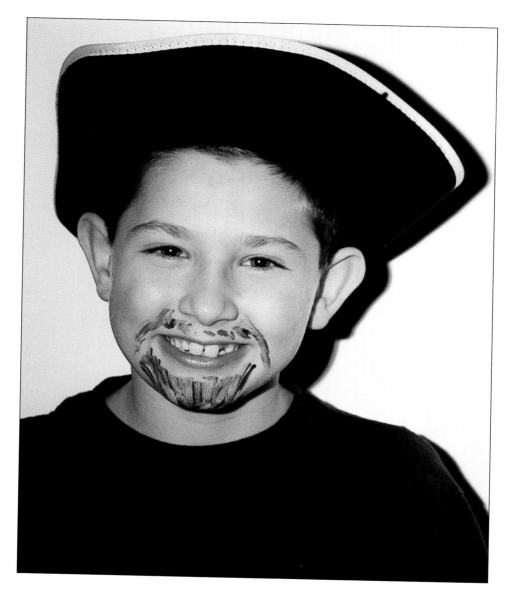

Jews remember how
their people were saved.
They celebrate their joy
on Purim.

Purim usually takes place
in March.

March 2011

Sunday	Monday	Tuesday	Wednesday	Thursday	Friday	Saturday
		1	2	3	4	5
6	7	8	9	10	11	12
13	14	15	16	17	18	19
20	21	22	23	24	25	26
27	28	29	30	31		

Many people wear
costumes on Purim.

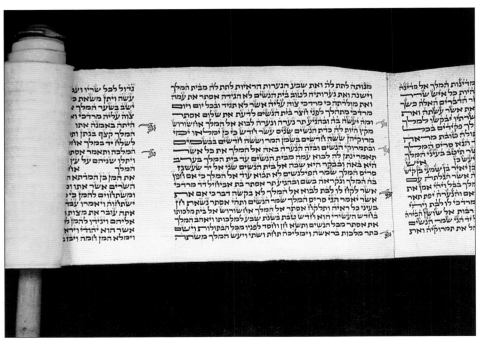

Scroll

They go to hear the story
of Esther. It is read from
a scroll called a Megillah
(meh-GEE-luh).

19

When Haman's name is read, everyone makes noise. Some hiss and boo. Other people shake rattles called groggers.

They make noise to show
that they do not like Haman.

There are parades on Purim.
They are lots of fun.

On Purim, families share
a big lunch called a seudah
(seh-oo-DAH).

Some take gift baskets to their friends. The gift baskets are called mishloach manot (meesh-LOW-ock mah-NOTE).

Hamantaschen (HAH-mahn-tah-shuhn) are special cookies. They are supposed to look like Haman's hat.

Charity (CHA-rih-tee) is also given to poor people. Charity is money, food, or other gifts given to poor people to help them.

Purim is a time to share with others.

Purim is fun!

It is a very happy
Jewish holiday.

Words You Know

charity

costumes

gift baskets

groggers

30

hamantaschen

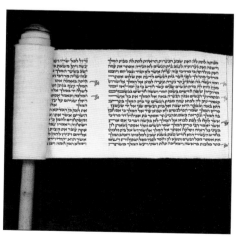

parades

scroll

seudah

Index

About the Author

Carmen Bredeson lives in Texas. She has written a number of books for children.

Photo Credits

Photographs © 2003: Corbis Images: 22, 31 top right (Gyori Antoine/Sygma), 16, 30 top right (Richard T. Nowitz), 28 (Moshe Shai); PhotoEdit/Bill Aron: cover, 25, 31 top left; Randy Matusow: 6, 9, 10, 13, 20, 23, 24, 30 bottom left, 30 bottom right, 31 bottom right; Richard Lobell Photography: 5, 18, 19, 21, 27, 30 top left, 31 bottom left; The Image Works/David Wells: 3.